Let's Match the Umbrellas

To Parents: This activity is designed to help your child differentiate between various colors and shapes. If your child does not recognize the pairs right away, ask him or her to describe the colors and patterns on the umbrellas.

Draw a line from each umbrella in the example box to its match.

Let's Match the Picnic Items

To Parents: With your child's help, point to and name each item in the example box. Then, do the activity. It is not important that your child draws a straight line. The goal is to match similar objects.

Draw a line from each picnic item in the example box to its match.

Let's Find Who's Hiding

To Parents: The focus of this activity is matching wholes with parts. First, guide your child to point to and name each animal in the example box (monkey, giraffe, elephant, snake, lion, rhinoceros, parrot).

Draw a line from each animal in the example box to where it is hiding in the picture.

4

Let's Find Who's Hiding

To Parents: In this activity, your child will match wholes with parts. First, guide your child to point to and name each animal in the example box (beetle, dragonfly, frog, grasshopper, fish, snail, tadpole, crayfish).

Draw a line from each animal in the example box to where it is hiding in the picture.

Let's Count Monkeys

To Parents: Have your child point to and count the monkeys inside the number 3. Emphasize that the number 3 represents three objects. Ask, "How many monkeys are inside the number?" Then, let your child choose a color to fill in the circles at the bottom of the page.

Count the monkeys inside the number **3**.

Then, color the same number of ◯ at the bottom.

Let's Count Cats

To Parents: Emphasize that the number 5 represents five objects. Ask, "How many cats are inside the number?" Then, let your child choose a color to fill in the circles at the bottom of the page.

Count the cats inside the number 5.

Then, color the same number of ◯ at the bottom.

Let's Count Giraffes

To Parents: This activity ties the idea of quantity (one) to the symbol that represents that quantity (1). Extend the activity by asking your child to trace the red box below.

Count the giraffes inside the number 1.

Then, color the same number of ◯ at the bottom.

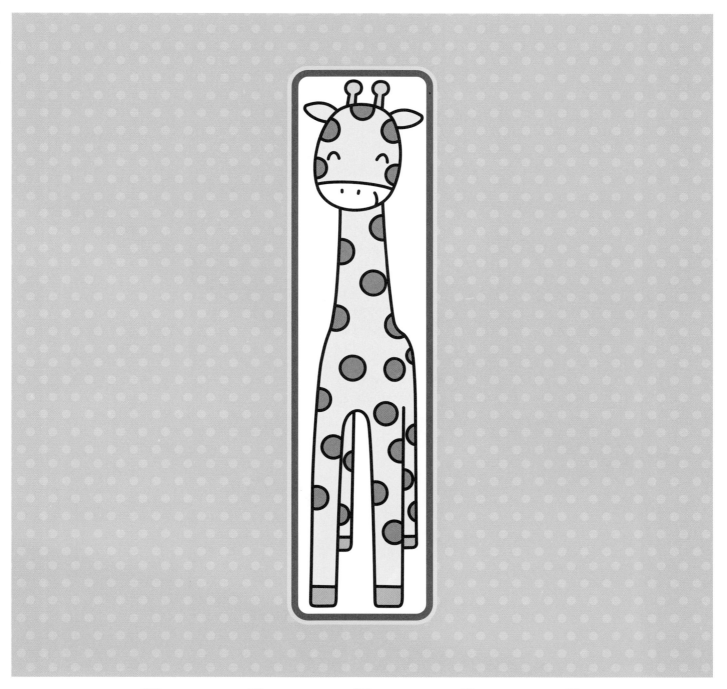

Let's Count Alligators

To Parents: After your child colors in the circles at the bottom of the page, extend the activity by asking your child to describe the alligators.

Count the alligators inside the number 4.

Then, color the same number of ◯ at the bottom.

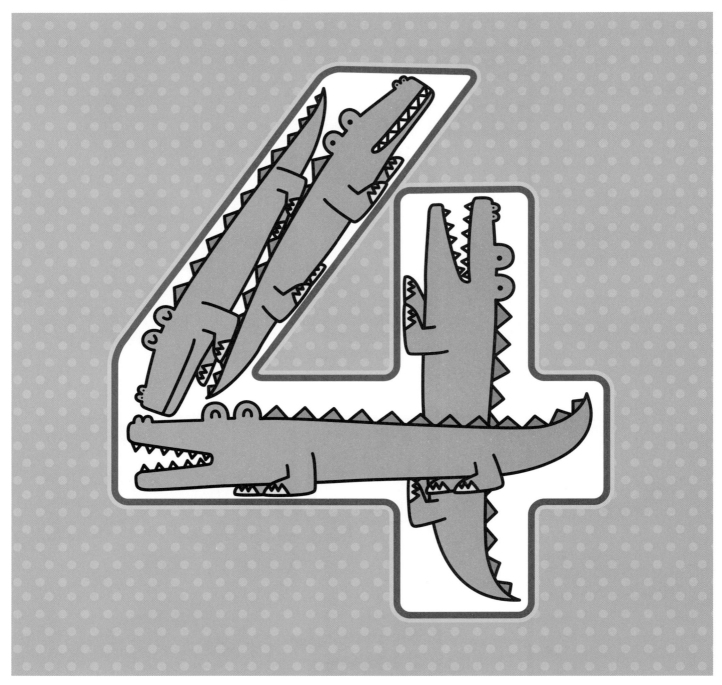

Let's Count Rabbits

To Parents: Let your child choose which color to use in the circles at the bottom of the page. Ask your child, "Have you ever seen a rabbit in real life?"

Count the rabbits inside the number 2.

Then, color the same number of ◯ at the bottom.

Let's Use Hat Stickers

To Parents: Have your child point to and count the four animals. Then, ask your child to put one hat sticker (from the front of the book) on the head of each animal. Help your child understand that there are four animals and four hats.

GOOD JOB!
Sticker

These animals want to wear hats. Put a hat sticker on each animal's head.

Let's Count by Twos

To Parents: This activity is designed to help children learn how to compare different quantities. Have your child point to and count each set of creepy creatures individually before comparing.

GOOD JOB!

Sticker

Draw a path from ➡ to ➡. At each split in the path, go in the direction of the group that has 2 creatures in it.

Let's Count by Threes

To Parents: Have your child point to and count each set of penguins. Next, have your child help the seals get past the penguins by drawing a line along the path of threes from ➡ to ➡.

Draw a path from ➡ to ➡. At each split in the path, go in the direction of the group that has 3 penguins in it.

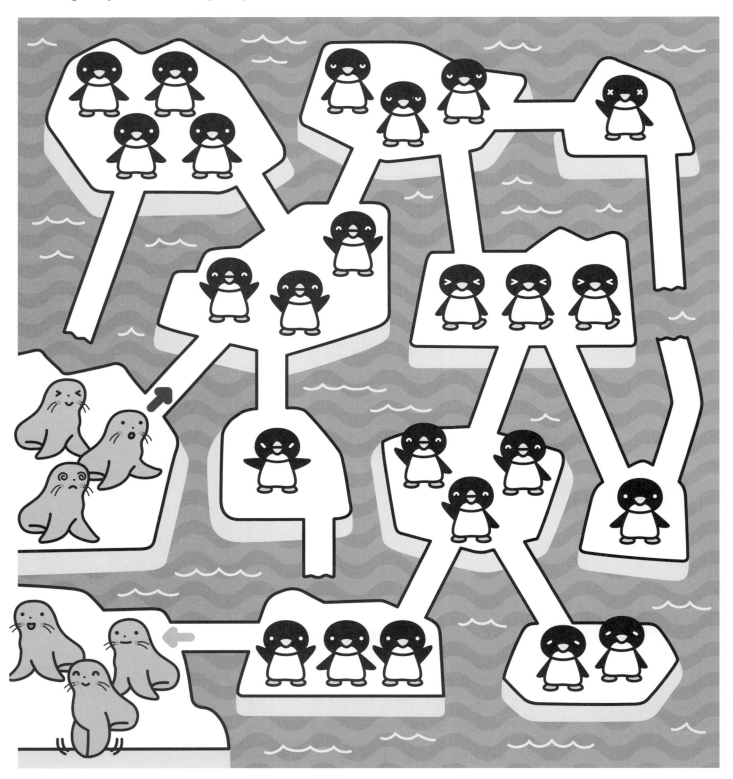

Let's Find Out Which Has More

To Parents: In this activity, your child will practice counting and comparing different quantities.

Count the candies in each jar. Then, color the ◯ under the jar with the most candies.

Let's Find Out Who Has More

To Parents: Here, your child will practice counting and comparing different quantities. Have your child point to and count each of the carrot sticks individually before comparing.

GOOD JOB!

Sticker

Count the carrot sticks on each place mat.

Then, color the ◯ under the place mat with the most carrot sticks.

Let's Match the Front and the Side of Cars

To Parents: This activity will help your child understand that an object has more than one side. Explain that the example box shows the front views of different vehicles, while side views of the same vehicles are below.

GOOD JOB!
Sticker

Draw a line to connect each vehicle with its match.

Let's Match the Front and the Side of Trains

To Parents: Explain that the example box shows the front views of different trains, while the side views of the same trains are shown on the right. Then, ask your child to draw a line from the front view of each train in the example box to the side view it matches.

GOOD JOB!
Sticker

Draw a line to connect each train with its match.

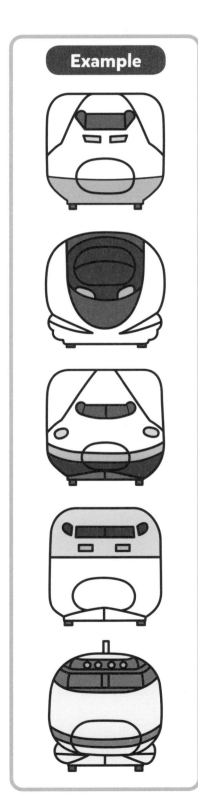

Example

Let's Match Animal Shapes and Shadows

To Parents: Discuss some of the identifying features of each animal's shape (the rabbit has long ears, the fox has a fluffy tail, the bear looks like he's waving). Then, ask your child to point to the shadow that matches each animal.

Find each animal's shadow. Draw a line from the animal to its shadow.

Let's Match Sea Shapes and Shadows

To Parents: Discuss some of the identifying features that each sea creature has (the turtle has a round shell, the octopus has eight legs, the crab has two sharp claws, the squid has two long tentacles). Then, ask your child to point to the shadow that matches each sea creature.

Find each animal's shadow. Draw a line from the animal to its shadow.

Let's Draw Using Shapes

To Parents: Encourage your child to draw original pictures and not to copy the images in the example box.

Use the shapes to draw anything you want.

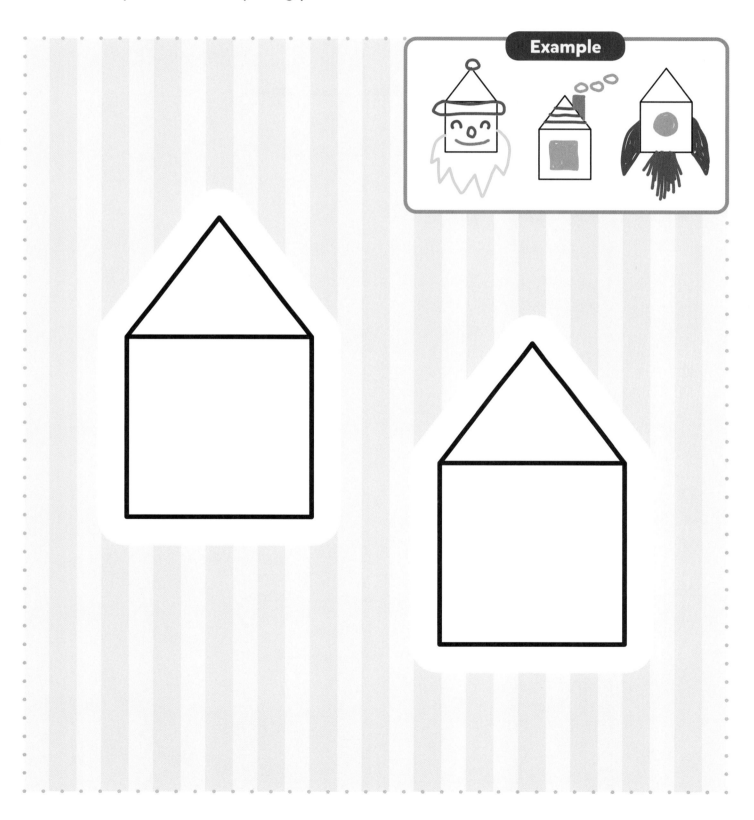

Example

Let's Draw Using Shapes

To Parents: Encourage your child to be creative and not just copy the pictures in the example box.

Use the shapes to draw anything you like.

Example

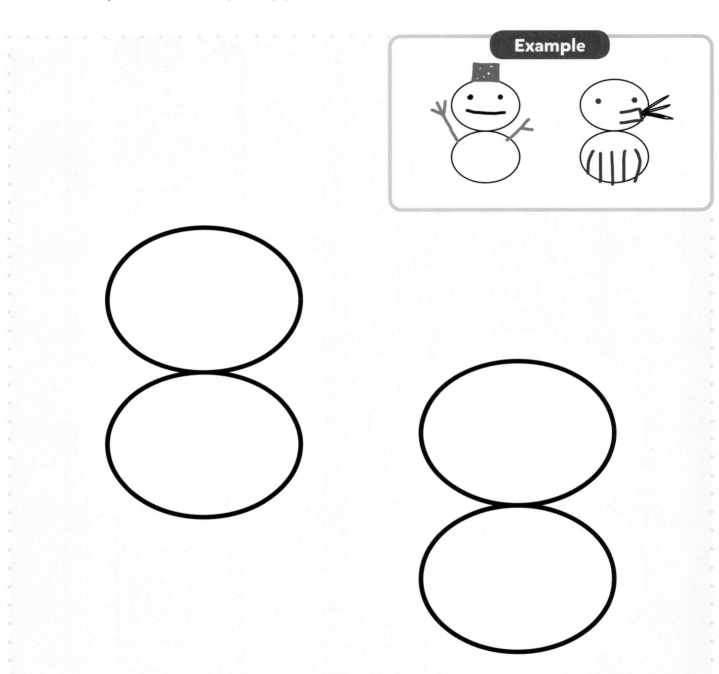

Let's Find Snacks

To Parents: Discuss the size, shape, and color of each snack in the example box. Then, have your child draw a line connecting each snack in the example box to its match in the tasty castle below.

GOOD JOB!

Sticker

Draw a line from each snack in the example box to its match in the picture.

Let's Match Beach Shapes

To Parents: Before your child does the activity, discuss the different shape outlines in the example box. Point out that the shapes in the example box are the same size, but not the same color, as the shapes in the picture.

Draw a line from each shape in the example box to its match in the picture.

Example

Let's Match Classroom Shapes

To Parents: Discuss the different shapes. After your child matches the objects, point to each shape and ask your child what it is.

Draw a line between each shape and the matching object in the picture below.

Let's Match Kitchen Shapes

To Parents: After your child has matched the objects, point to each shape and ask your child what it is.

Draw a line between each shape and the matching object in the picture below.

Let's Draw an Angry Face

To Parents: After completing the activity, have your child draw the face of a happy cat on another piece of paper.

Draw an angry cat with two eyes, a nose, and a mouth.

Example

Let's Draw a Sad Face

To Parents: After completing the activity, have your child draw the face of a sleepy dog or a laughing dog on another piece of paper.

Draw a crying dog with two eyes, a nose, and a mouth.

Example

GOOD JOB!

Sticker

Let's Compare Sizes

To Parents: In this activity, your child will compare three different sizes. Then, ask your child which of the houses is the second largest.

Circle the largest house. Draw a △ around the smallest house.

Let's Compare Sizes

To Parents: In this activity, your child will take note of size differences among objects. Ask your child which of the turtles is the second smallest.

Circle the largest turtle. Draw a △ around the smallest turtle.

Let's Draw Patterns

To Parents: Have your child draw a pattern of his or her choosing on the butterfly's wings and color the flowers any color. Explain that the example box may help to give your child ideas, but it is not meant to be copied exactly.

Draw patterns on the butterfly's wings. Color the flowers.

Example

Let's Draw Patterns

To Parents: Have your child use crayons, markers, or colored pencils to decorate the princess's dress. Make sure your child knows to draw whatever she or he likes.

GOOD JOB!
Sticker

Draw patterns on the princess's dress.

Example

Let's Trace a Face

To Parents: Have your child use a pencil, crayon, or marker to trace the girl's hair, eyes, and mouth. Encourage your child to follow the lines as closely as possible. Then, have him or her put the bow stickers anywhere on the page.

Trace the gray dotted lines. Then, put the bow stickers on the picture.

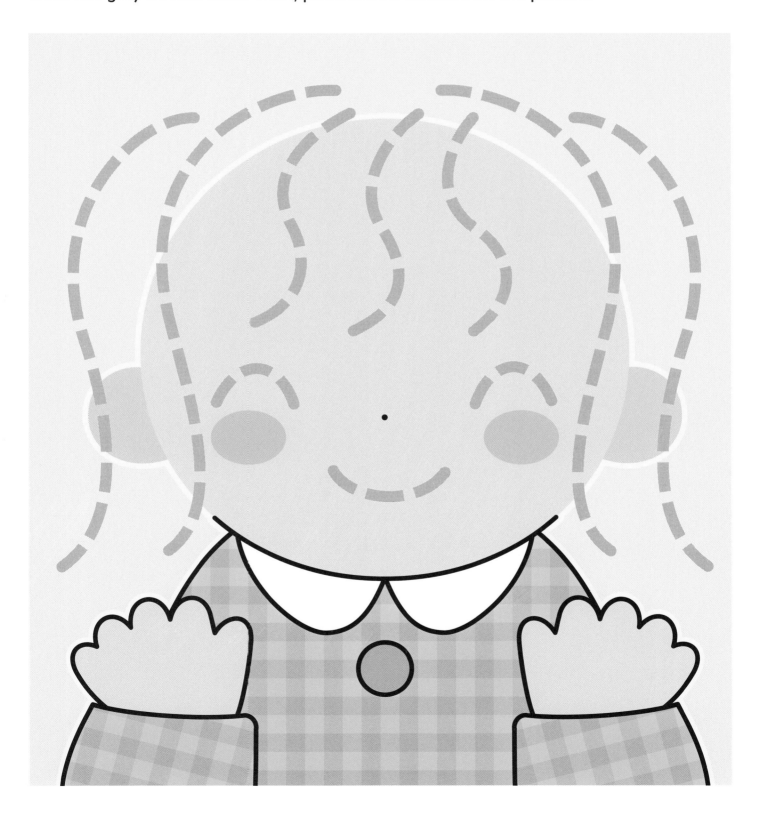

Let's Trace a Face

To Parents: Encourage your child to follow the lines as closely as possible. Then, have him or her put the mustache sticker anywhere on the page.

Trace the gray dotted lines. Then, put the mustache sticker on the picture.

Let's Practice Being Polite

To Parents: Point to the top picture and ask, "What do you say when you wake up in the morning?" Then, point to the bottom picture and ask, "What do you say just before you go to sleep at night?"

Pretend you just woke up. What do you do? Then, pretend you are about to go to sleep.

Let's Use Utensils

To Parents: After your child says each correct answer, have him or her apply the appropriate utensil sticker from the front of the book (the fork for the spaghetti and the spoons for the cereal and ice cream).

What utensil do you use to eat each food below? Name it.

Then, put the matching sticker in each child's hand.

Sticker

SPAGHETTI

Sticker

CEREAL

Sticker

ICE CREAM

Let's Use Store Stickers

Sticker

GOOD JOB!

Sticker

Put the store stickers around the town in the picture below.

Let's Say Which Food Comes First

To Parents: Say, "At dinnertime, salad is often eaten first, meat and vegetables next, and dessert last." When all the stickers are on the plate, ask your child what is eaten first, next, and last. Then, ask, "What is your favorite food?"

Put the dinner foods in the tray in the order you eat them.

Let's Say What Comes First

To Parents: Ask your child what comes first: finishing dinner or getting dessert. Point out the order in the picture and say, "First, you finish eating your dinner. Next, you get dessert."

Point to the picture that comes first.

That was delicious. Thank you.

Now I can have dessert!

Let's Go Shopping

Tell a story about the girl and her mom going shopping.

Let's Find the Matches

To Parents: Ask your child to help you determine which watermelon is the largest. Explain that the largest watermelon goes in the largest box and so on. Have your child draw a line between the dots to match each watermelon with its box.

Draw a line to connect each watermelon with the box that matches its size.

Put sticker faces on the watermelons.

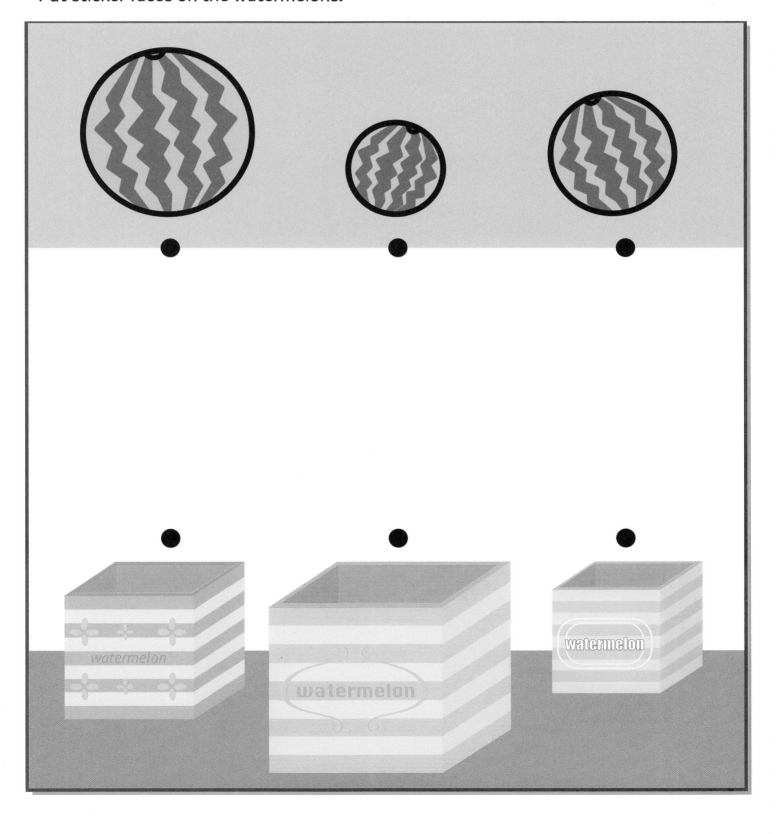

Let's Find Out How Chickens Grow

To Parents: This activity is designed to teach the life cycle of a chicken. As your child follows the path, explain how a baby chicken is hatched from an egg, grows into a chick, and finally develops into an adult chicken.

GOOD JOB!
Sticker

Draw a path through the maze from ➡ to ➡.

Let's Find Out How Butterflies Grow

To Parents: This activity is designed to teach the life cycle of a butterfly. As your child follows the path, explain how a butterfly begins as an egg, becomes a larva, then a pupa, and finally a beautiful butterfly.

GOOD JOB!

Sticker

Draw a path through the maze from ➡ to ➡.

EGG

LARVA

PUPA

BUTTERFLY

Let's Find Out How Beetles Grow

To Parents: This activity is designed to teach the life cycle of a beetle. As your child follows the path, explain how a beetle begins as an egg, becomes a larva, then a pupa, and finally an adult beetle. Be sure to point out the animals and insects from the book when you see them in nature.

Draw a path through the maze from ➡ to ➡.

Let's Find Out How Sea Turtles Grow

To Parents: As your child follows the path, explain how sea turtles start out as eggs, then hatch as baby turtles, and finally grow into adult sea turtles. Extend the learning by asking what other animals your child sees on the page.

Draw a path through the maze from ➡ to ➡.

Let's Find the Matching Socks

To Parents: To find the matches, remind your child to pay special attention to each sock's color, pattern, and length.

Draw lines to connect the matching socks.

Let's Find the Matching Aprons

To Parents: To find the pairs, remind your child to pay special attention to each apron's color and pattern. The length does not matter.

Draw lines to connect the matching aprons.

Let's Put Seeds in the Watermelon

Sticker

To Parents: Use the seed stickers from the front of the book. Extend the learning by asking your child to count the number of seeds.

Put the seed stickers on the watermelon in any pattern you like.

Example

Let's Brush Our Teeth

To Parents: Have your child help you fold the page according to the instructions. Then, say, "What is the boy doing?" (He is brushing his teeth.) Allow your child to fold and unfold the page many times to enjoy the change in pictures.

GOOD JOB!
Sticker

Cut along the ▬▬ line. Fold the page to see what the boy is doing.

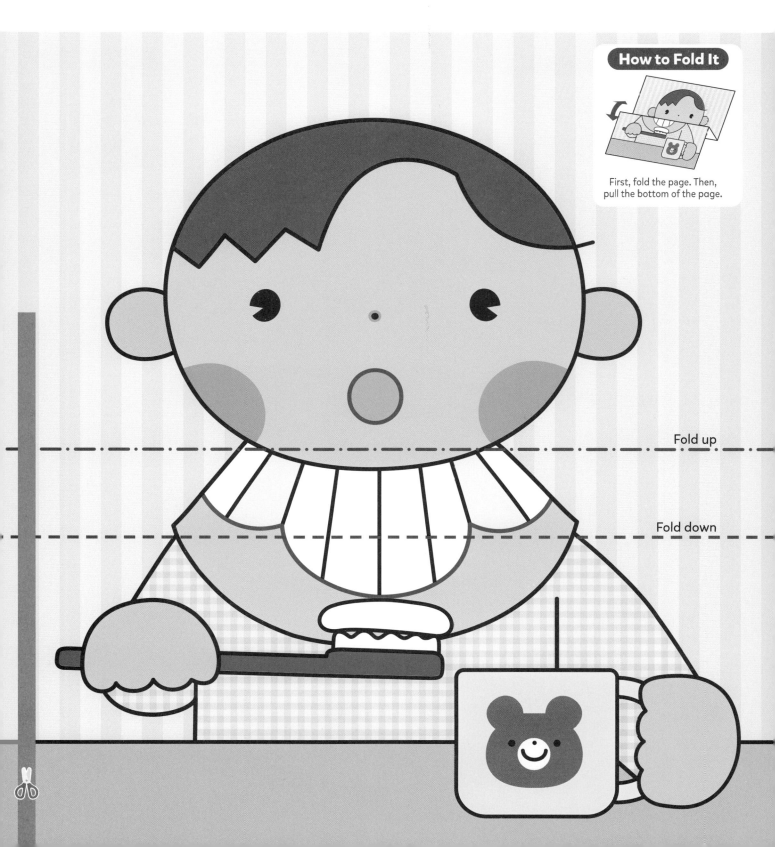

How to Fold It

First, fold the page. Then, pull the bottom of the page.

Fold up

Fold down

Let's Help Bear Fix His Teeth

To Parents: Say, "Bear lost all of his teeth because he didn't brush them. Let's give Bear new teeth." Then, have your child help you fold the page according to the instructions.

Apply stickers to help Bear fix his teeth.

Then, cut along the ▬▬ line and fold the page.

How to Fold It

First, fold the page. Then, pull the bottom of the page.

sticker

sticker

Fold down

Fold up

GOOD JOB!
Sticker

Let's Draw Fruit Faces

To Parents: Encourage your child to draw faces that express different feelings (happy, sad, sleepy, angry, etc.).

Draw a face on each piece of fruit.

Example

Let's Color the Robot

To Parents: Explain to your child that the example box is only for ideas. It is not meant to be copied exactly.

Draw a face and patterns on the robot.

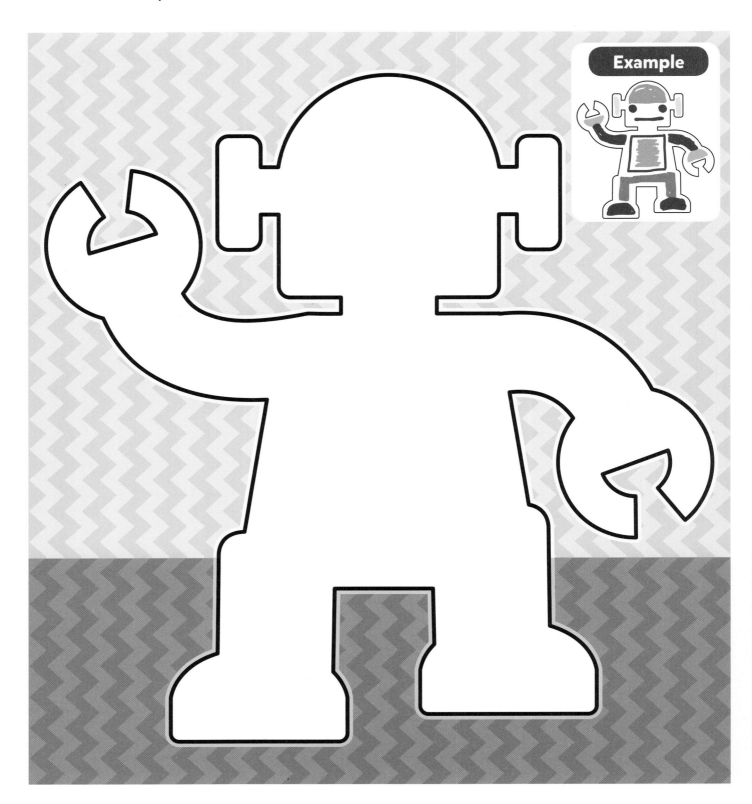

Example

Let's Trace the Letter A

To Parents: From this page to page 54, your child will learn to write the letters of the alphabet. First, have your child slowly trace the letter with his or her finger several times. Then, you might have your child trace the letter with a crayon.

Trace the letter A with your finger. Then, say its name.

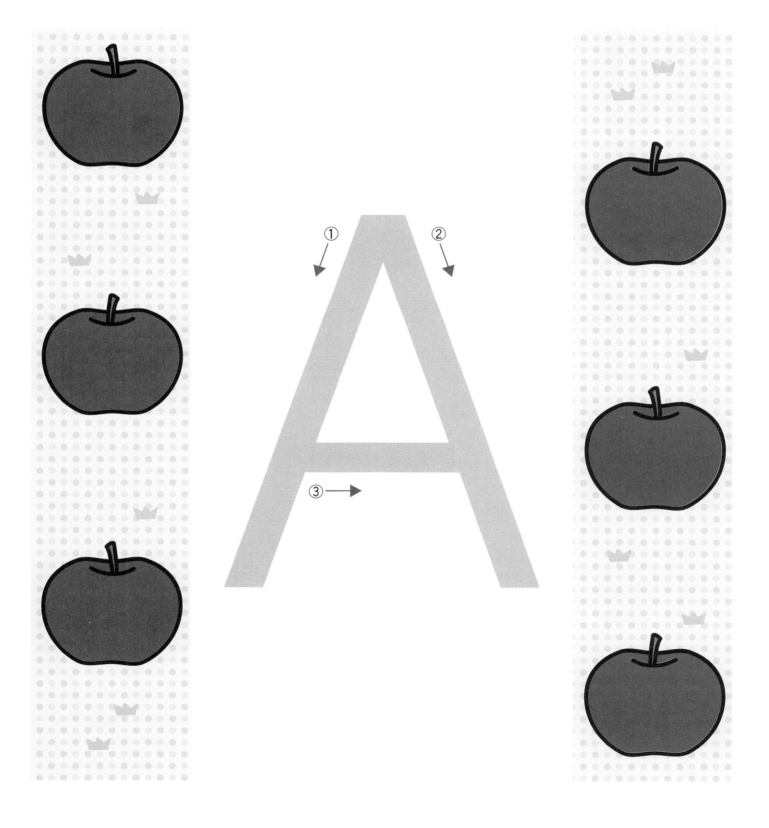

GOOD JOB!

Sticker

Let's Trace the Letter B

To Parents: When your child is tracing each letter, make sure he or she follows the arrows in order.

Trace the letter B with your finger. Then, say its name.

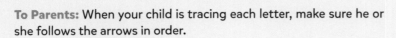

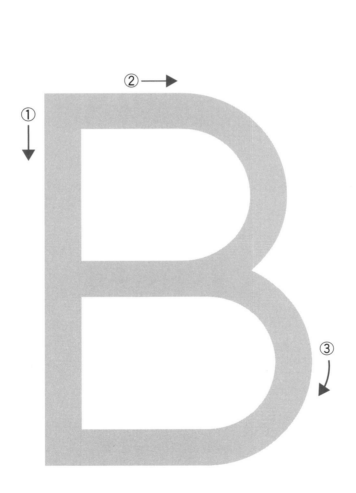

Let's Trace the Letter C

To Parents: After your child traces the letter, say, "*C* is for *cat*."

Trace the letter C with your finger. Then, say its name.

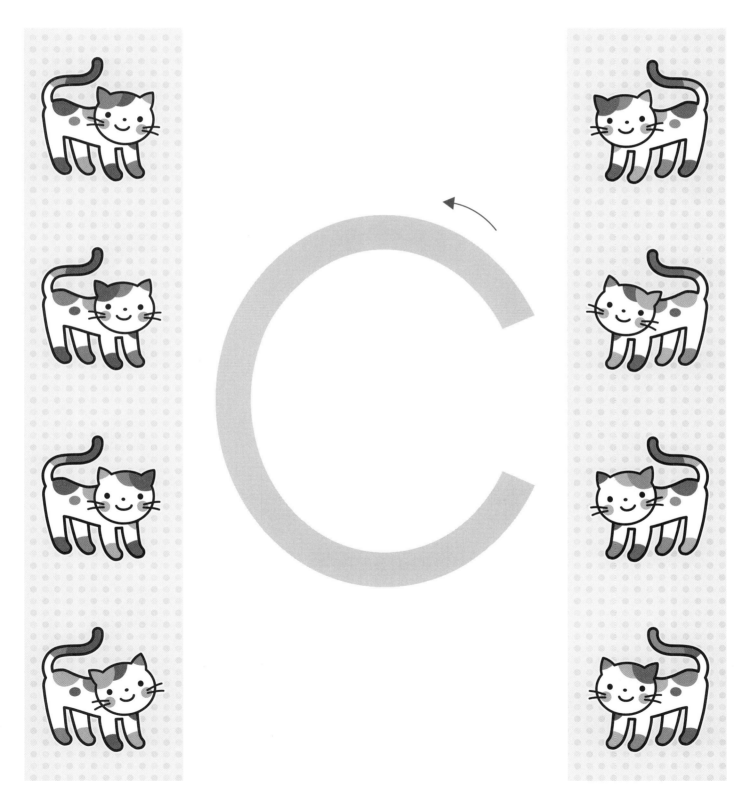

Let's Trace the Letter D

To Parents: Make sure your child draws the lines in order. After your child traces the letter, say, "*D* is for *dog.*"

GOOD JOB!
Sticker

Trace the letter D with your finger. Then, say its name.

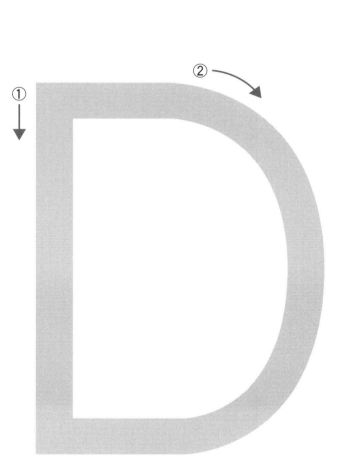

Let's Match the Parts

To Parents: After your child has finished connecting the objects, ask him or her to name the animal and the body part.

Draw a line to connect each body part in the example box with the matching animal in the picture.

Let's Match the Instruments

To Parents: After your child has finished matching the instruments, ask her or him to name each instrument and act out what kind of sound it makes. Help your child with the names if she or he does not know them.

GOOD JOB!

Sticker

Draw a line to connect each musical instrument in the example box with its match in the picture.

Example

TRUMPET

HARMONICA

DRUM

CYMBALS

RECORDER

Let's Match Pairs of Glasses

To Parents: Using the stickers from the front of the book, have your child apply a pair of glasses to each face. Ask, "Which pair of glasses do you think would look nice on this person?"

GOOD JOB!

Sticker

Put a pair of glasses on each person's face.

Let's Play with Hamsters

To Parents: Using the stickers from the front of the book, have your child apply one hamster sticker to each activity below. As your child takes each sticker off the sticker page, ask, "What is this hamster doing?" and "Where do you think it best fits in the picture?"

Put the hamster stickers where they best fit in the pictures below.

Let's Go Through the Maze

To Parents: Guide your child to make sharp points at each turn as he or she draws a path through the zigzag maze.

Draw a path through the maze from 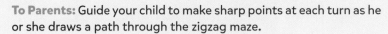 to .

Let's Figure Out What Doesn't Belong

To Parents: Ask your child to name each object in the picture below. Then, ask which three objects do not belong and why. If your child is having a hard time, direct him or her to look for things that are not vegetables.

Circle **3** objects that do not belong in the picture.

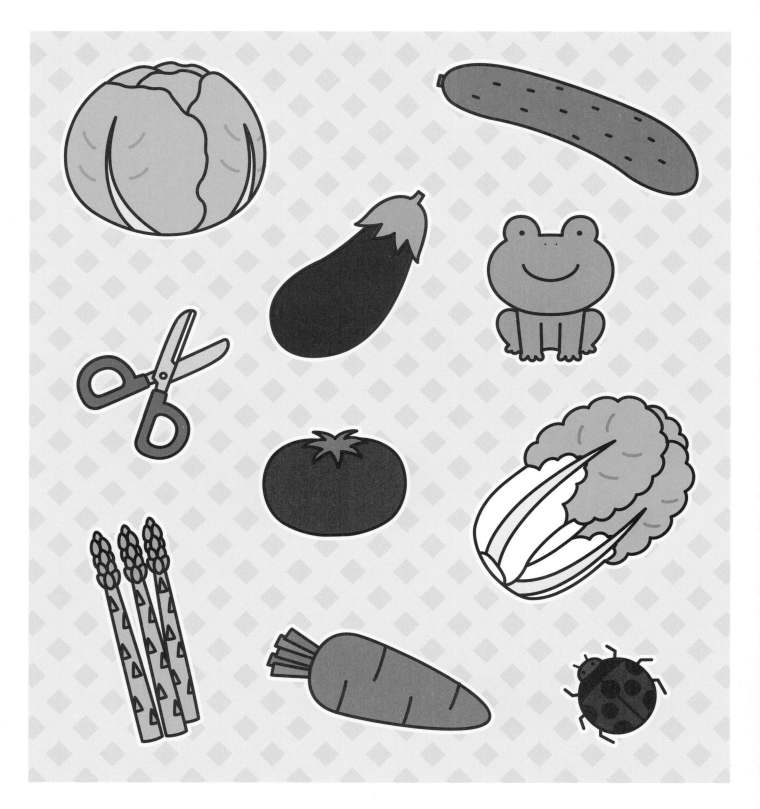

Let's Figure Out Which Path to Take

To Parents: Mazes train your child to look for possible problems or obstacles and find ways around them.

Draw a path through the dinosaur maze from ➡ to ➡.

Let's Figure Out Which Path to Take

To Parents: To get through this maze, your child will use reasoning and problem-solving skills. Help him or her draw a path through the maze without hitting a dead end.

Draw a path through the rabbit maze from to ➡.

Let's Finish the Picture

To Parents: If your child is not sure where to put the cutouts, ask him or her to describe what is in each picture.

GOOD JOB!
Sticker

Cut out the pictures at the bottom of the page and glue them on the ☐ boxes to complete the picture.

GLUE
For
page 64

GLUE
For
page 64

Let's Finish the Picture

To Parents: If your child is not sure where to put the cutouts, ask her or him to describe what is happening in each picture.

Cut out the pictures at the bottom of the page and glue them on the boxes to finish the picture.

GLUE
For
page 63

GLUE
For
page 63